EMMANUEL JOSEPH

Brainwaves and Beats, Exploring the Neuroscience and Anthropology of Music

Copyright © 2025 by Emmanuel Joseph

All rights reserved. No part of this publication may be reproduced, stored or transmitted in any form or by any means, electronic, mechanical, photocopying, recording, scanning, or otherwise without written permission from the publisher. It is illegal to copy this book, post it to a website, or distribute it by any other means without permission.

First edition

This book was professionally typeset on Reedsy.
Find out more at reedsy.com

Contents

1	Chapter 1: The Origins of Music	1
2	Chapter 2: The Neuroscience of Music Perception	3
3	Chapter 3: Music and Emotion	5
4	Chapter 4: The Cultural Significance of Music	7
5	Chapter 5: The Evolution of Musical Instruments	9
6	Chapter 6: Music and Dance	11
7	Chapter 7: The Science of Rhythm	13
8	Chapter 8: Music and Memory	15
9	Chapter 9: Music and Technology	17
10	Chapter 10: The Psychology of Music	19
11	Chapter 11: The Globalization of Music	21
12	Chapter 12: The Future of Music	23
13	Chapter 13: Music and Identity	25
14	Chapter 14: Music and Healing	27
15	Chapter 15: The Philosophy of Music	29

1

Chapter 1: The Origins of Music

Music, in all its diverse forms, has been an integral part of human culture since the dawn of civilization. The journey of music begins with our earliest ancestors, who may have discovered rhythm through the natural sounds around them - the beating of sticks, the rustling of leaves, and the melodies of birds. These primal sounds likely sparked the first musical expressions, deeply intertwined with rituals and communal activities. As early humans evolved, so did their musicality, leading to the creation of rudimentary instruments like drums and flutes, which paved the way for more complex musical traditions.

Anthropologists have long studied the origins of music to understand its role in human evolution. They believe that music was not just a form of entertainment but served vital functions in social cohesion and communication. Singing and dancing around the fire would have strengthened group bonds, while rhythmic chants and drumming could coordinate communal activities like hunting and farming. Over time, these early musical practices would become deeply embedded in the cultural fabric of societies, reflecting their values, beliefs, and histories.

The development of music can be seen in the rich tapestries of ancient civilizations. In Mesopotamia, the earliest known musical notation dates back to around 1400 BCE, revealing a sophisticated understanding of musical scales and harmonies. Similarly, ancient Egypt, Greece, and China had well-established musical traditions that played crucial roles in their religious and social ceremonies. These early examples demonstrate how music transcends mere sound, becoming a powerful medium for storytelling and cultural expression.

Despite the vast differences in musical styles across the globe, the fundamental human connection to music remains universal. From the haunting melodies of Native American flutes to the complex rhythms of African drums, music speaks to the core of our shared humanity. By exploring the origins of music, we gain insight into the ways it has shaped our past and continues to influence our lives today.

2

Chapter 2: The Neuroscience of Music Perception

The human brain is remarkably attuned to music, processing its various elements with a precision that is still not fully understood. Neuroscientists have discovered that listening to music engages multiple brain regions, including those responsible for auditory processing, emotion, and memory. When we hear a familiar song, our auditory cortex decodes the sound waves, while the limbic system, which is involved in emotion, reacts to the music's emotional content. This intricate interplay of neural networks explains why music can evoke such powerful and varied emotional responses.

Research has shown that music activates the brain's reward system, releasing neurotransmitters like dopamine, which creates feelings of pleasure and satisfaction. This response is similar to the one triggered by other rewarding activities, such as eating or socializing. It is this connection between music and the brain's reward system that underlies our deep-seated love for music and its ability to lift our spirits or soothe our minds in times of stress.

Moreover, the study of music perception has revealed fascinating insights into the brain's ability to recognize and predict patterns. When we listen to a piece of music, our brain is constantly making predictions about what will come next based on its understanding of musical structure. This predictive coding mechanism allows us to anticipate musical phrases and harmonies, enhancing our enjoyment of the music when our expectations are met or pleasantly surprised.

The therapeutic potential of music has also been a subject of extensive research. Music therapy has been shown to have positive effects on individuals with neurological disorders, such as Parkinson's disease and Alzheimer's disease. For example, rhythmic auditory stimulation can help improve motor function in Parkinson's patients, while familiar songs can trigger memories and emotional responses in individuals with Alzheimer's, providing a sense of connection and comfort.

3

Chapter 3: Music and Emotion

The relationship between music and emotion is complex and multifaceted, deeply rooted in both our biology and cultural context. Music has the unique ability to convey and evoke a wide range of emotions, from joy and excitement to sadness and nostalgia. This emotional power of music is evident in its use across various cultural rituals, celebrations, and personal experiences.

At the biological level, music's emotional impact can be attributed to its effect on the brain's limbic system, which is responsible for processing emotions. When we listen to music, our brain releases neurotransmitters like dopamine and oxytocin, which contribute to the feelings of pleasure and bonding. This neurochemical response explains why certain songs can make us feel euphoric or bring tears to our eyes.

Culturally, music plays a vital role in expressing and reinforcing collective emotions. In many societies, music is an essential part of religious ceremonies, festivals, and communal gatherings. These musical traditions provide a shared emotional experience that strengthens social bonds and fosters a sense of belonging. For example, the rhythmic chants and drumming in African rituals create a powerful collective energy that unites participants, while the melancholic melodies of traditional Irish music evoke a deep sense of nostalgia and longing.

The emotional power of music is also harnessed in various forms of media, such as film, television, and advertising. Composers and sound designers carefully craft musical scores to enhance the emotional impact of a scene, guiding the audience's feelings and reactions. A suspenseful soundtrack can heighten tension in a thriller, while a tender piano piece can evoke feelings of love and intimacy in a romance.

Understanding the connection between music and emotion provides valuable insights into its therapeutic potential. Music therapy has been used to address a wide range of emotional and psychological issues, from anxiety and depression to trauma and grief. By tapping into the emotional power of music, therapists can help individuals process their feelings, express themselves, and find a sense of solace and healing.

4

Chapter 4: The Cultural Significance of Music

Music is a universal language that transcends geographical, linguistic, and cultural boundaries. Throughout history, it has played a crucial role in shaping and reflecting the identities of communities and societies. From traditional folk songs to contemporary pop hits, music serves as a powerful medium for storytelling, cultural expression, and social cohesion.

In many indigenous cultures, music is deeply intertwined with oral traditions and serves as a means of preserving and transmitting knowledge. Songs and chants are used to recount historical events, convey moral lessons, and celebrate significant life events. For example, the Australian Aboriginal songlines are musical maps that encode information about the landscape, guiding travelers across vast distances. Similarly, the griots of West Africa are oral historians who use music to recount the histories and genealogies of their people.

Music also plays a vital role in religious and spiritual practices around the world. Sacred music, from Gregorian chants to Sufi qawwali, creates a sense of reverence and connection to the divine. These musical traditions often involve intricate rituals and performances that bring communities together in shared worship and devotion. The transcendental experience of sacred music can evoke profound emotions and a sense of spiritual transcendence.

The cultural significance of music extends to its role in social and political movements. Throughout history, music has been a powerful tool for protest and social change. Protest songs and anthems have rallied people together, giving voice to their struggles and aspirations. For instance, the civil rights movement in the United States was accompanied by powerful songs like "We Shall Overcome" that inspired and united activists in their fight for justice and equality.

Moreover, music reflects and shapes the values, identities, and aspirations of contemporary societies. In the modern era, genres like hip-hop, rock, and electronic music have given rise to vibrant subcultures and global movements. These musical genres provide a platform for artists to address social issues, challenge norms, and express their individuality. Music festivals, concerts, and online platforms further amplify these cultural expressions, creating spaces for diverse voices to be heard.

By exploring the cultural significance of music, we gain a deeper appreciation of its role in shaping human experiences and fostering a sense of belonging and identity.

5

Chapter 5: The Evolution of Musical Instruments

The history of musical instruments is a testament to human creativity and innovation. From the simplest percussive tools made of bones and stones to the complex electronic instruments of today, the evolution of musical instruments reflects our enduring fascination with sound and our desire to push the boundaries of musical expression.

One of the earliest known musical instruments is the bone flute, dating back over 40,000 years. These ancient flutes, crafted from bird bones and mammoth ivory, suggest that early humans had a sophisticated understanding of pitch and rhythm. As civilizations developed, so did their instruments. The Sumerians, for example, created the lyre and harp, while the ancient Egyptians developed wind instruments like the flute and trumpet.

The Middle Ages and the Renaissance saw significant advancements in instrument design and construction. The development of string instruments, such as the violin and lute, allowed for greater musical complexity and expression. The invention of the pipe organ and clavichord laid the foundation for the modern piano, transforming the landscape of Western classical music. These innovations were driven by both cultural influences and technological advancements, as instrument makers experimented with new materials and techniques.

The 20th century brought about a revolution in musical instruments with the advent of electronic technology. The invention of the electric guitar, synthesizer, and digital sampler opened up new possibilities for sound creation and manipulation. Electronic instruments have become central to many modern music genres, from rock and pop to electronic dance music (EDM). Today, the fusion of traditional and electronic instruments continues to push the boundaries of musical creativity, reflecting the dynamic and ever-evolving nature of music.

The evolution of musical instruments is not just a story of technological progress but also a reflection of cultural exchange. As societies interacted through trade, conquest, and migration, they shared their musical traditions and instruments. The sitar from India, the koto from Japan, and the djembe from West Africa are just a few examples of how musical instruments have traveled across continents, enriching the global musical landscape.

6

Chapter 6: Music and Dance

Music and dance are intrinsically linked, with each form enhancing and complementing the other. Throughout history, dance has been an essential part of human culture, often serving as a physical expression of musical rhythms and melodies. The interplay between music and dance creates a dynamic and immersive experience, engaging both the performers and the audience.

In many cultures, dance is deeply rooted in tradition and ceremony. For example, the intricate footwork and rhythmic movements of Indian classical dance, such as Bharatanatyam and Kathak, are performed to the accompaniment of traditional music. These dance forms not only showcase the performers' skill and grace but also convey stories and emotions through their gestures and expressions. Similarly, the energetic and communal nature of African dance, often accompanied by drumming and chanting, reflects the cultural importance of rhythm and unity.

The relationship between music and dance is also evident in social and popular contexts. Ballroom dances, such as the waltz, tango, and salsa, have long been associated with specific musical styles and rhythms. These partner dances require synchronization and coordination, creating a harmonious connection between the dancers and the music. In contemporary dance, genres like hip-hop, breakdancing, and jazz dance have emerged alongside corresponding musical styles, each influencing and inspiring the other.

Dance and music also play a crucial role in theatrical and cinematic performances. In musical theater and ballet, the choreography is intricately tied to the musical score, enhancing the narrative and emotional impact of the performance. Film scores and soundtracks often include dance scenes, where the movement of the characters is choreographed to the music, creating memorable and iconic moments.

The synergy between music and dance is a testament to the power of artistic expression. Together, they create a multisensory experience that transcends linguistic and cultural barriers, allowing people to connect and communicate on a deeply emotional level.

7

Chapter 7: The Science of Rhythm

Rhythm is a fundamental element of music, providing structure and coherence to musical compositions. The science of rhythm explores how humans perceive, process, and produce rhythmic patterns, shedding light on the cognitive and neurological mechanisms underlying our sense of timing.

At its core, rhythm involves the organization of sounds and silences into a temporal framework. This temporal structure is often defined by a regular pulse or beat, which listeners can perceive and anticipate. The ability to synchronize with a beat is a remarkable human trait, enabling us to move, dance, and play music in unison with others.

Neuroscientists have identified specific brain regions involved in rhythm perception and production. The basal ganglia, a group of nuclei located deep within the brain, play a crucial role in timing and motor coordination. Research has shown that the basal ganglia are active when individuals tap their fingers to a beat or perform rhythmic movements. Additionally, the auditory and motor cortices are involved in processing and synchronizing rhythmic patterns, highlighting the interconnected nature of auditory and motor systems in rhythm perception.

Rhythmic entrainment, the phenomenon of synchronizing one's movements to an external rhythm, is a key aspect of musical performance and dance. This ability is not unique to humans; some animals, such as birds and primates, have also demonstrated rhythmic entrainment. However, humans exhibit a particularly high degree of rhythmic flexibility and complexity, allowing us to engage in a wide range of rhythmic activities.

The study of rhythm extends beyond music and dance, encompassing various aspects of human behavior and cognition. For instance, rhythmic patterns are evident in speech and language, where the timing and intonation of words convey meaning and emotion. Rhythmic coordination is also essential in activities like sports and teamwork, where precise timing and synchronization are crucial for success.

Understanding the science of rhythm provides insights into the cognitive and neural processes that underpin our ability to perceive and produce rhythmic patterns. This knowledge has practical applications in fields such as music education, therapy, and rehabilitation, where rhythm-based interventions can enhance learning, motor skills, and overall well-being.

8

Chapter 8: Music and Memory

Music has a profound impact on memory, with the ability to evoke vivid recollections and emotions from our past. The connection between music and memory is evident in everyday experiences, such as hearing a song that reminds us of a specific moment in our lives or a melody that triggers a flood of nostalgic memories.

The brain's ability to link music with memories is rooted in the close relationship between the auditory cortex and the hippocampus, a brain region involved in memory formation and retrieval. When we listen to music, the auditory cortex processes the sound, while the hippocampus associates the music with specific events, people, and emotions. This neural connection explains why certain songs can transport us back in time, allowing us to relive past experiences with remarkable clarity.

Research has shown that music can enhance memory and learning in various contexts. For example, studies have found that listening to background music while studying can improve focus and retention of information. Additionally, musical training has been associated with enhanced cognitive abilities, such as memory, attention, and problem-solving skills. These findings highlight the potential of music as a tool for cognitive development and educational enrichment.

Music's impact on memory is particularly significant in the context of aging and neurological disorders. Music therapy has been used to support individuals with Alzheimer's disease and other forms of dementia, helping to stimulate memories and improve cognitive function. Familiar songs and melodies can elicit emotional responses and memories that are otherwise inaccessible, providing comfort and a sense of connection for individuals with memory impairments.

The relationship between music and memory also extends to cultural and collective memories. National anthems, folk songs, and popular music serve as repositories of cultural heritage and shared experiences. These musical traditions carry the collective memories of communities, preserving their histories, values, and identities. By exploring the connection between music and memory, we gain a deeper understanding of how music shapes our individual and collective experiences, enriching our lives and fostering a sense of continuity and belonging.

9

Chapter 9: Music and Technology

The relationship between music and technology is a dynamic and evolving one, transforming the way we create, distribute, and experience music. From the invention of the phonograph to the rise of digital streaming platforms, technological advancements have continually reshaped the musical landscape.

The early 20th century saw the introduction of recording technology, which revolutionized the music industry by enabling the mass production and distribution of music. The phonograph, and later the gramophone, allowed people to listen to music in their homes, bringing the performances of renowned artists to audiences far and wide. This era also witnessed the birth of radio broadcasting, further expanding the reach of music and creating a shared cultural experience.

The mid-20th century brought about significant innovations in electronic music. The development of synthesizers, drum machines, and multi-track recording techniques opened up new possibilities for sound creation and manipulation. Artists and composers began experimenting with electronic instruments, giving rise to genres like electronic, techno, and house music. These advancements also influenced traditional music genres, leading to the emergence of new sounds and styles.

The digital age has had a profound impact on the music industry, transforming the way we consume and interact with music. The advent of the internet and digital distribution platforms has democratized access to music, allowing independent artists to share their work with a global audience. Streaming services, such as Spotify and Apple Music, have become the primary mode of music consumption, providing listeners with vast libraries of music at their fingertips.

Technology has also revolutionized the way music is produced and performed. Digital audio workstations (DAWs) and music production software have made it possible for artists to create and edit music with unprecedented precision and ease. Live performances have been enhanced by sophisticated sound systems, lighting effects, and visual projections, creating immersive and multisensory experiences for audiences.

As technology continues to advance, the future of music holds exciting possibilities. Virtual reality (VR) and augmented reality (AR) are already being used to create interactive and immersive musical experiences. Artificial intelligence (AI) is being explored for its potential to assist in composition, production, and personalized music recommendations. The synergy between music and technology promises to push the boundaries of creativity and redefine our relationship with music.

10

Chapter 10: The Psychology of Music

The psychology of music explores the ways in which music affects our thoughts, feelings, and behaviors. It delves into the cognitive and emotional processes that underlie our musical experiences, shedding light on why music holds such a powerful and universal appeal.

One area of interest in the psychology of music is the concept of musical preference. Why do we gravitate towards certain genres or artists? Research suggests that musical preferences are influenced by a combination of factors, including personality traits, cultural background, and life experiences. For example, individuals with high levels of openness to experience may be more inclined to explore diverse and unconventional music styles, while those with a strong sense of nostalgia may prefer songs from their formative years.

Another intriguing aspect is the role of music in regulating emotions. Many people turn to music to cope with stress, sadness, or anxiety. Listening to calming and soothing music can have a therapeutic effect, helping to reduce tension and promote relaxation. Conversely, energetic and upbeat music can boost mood and motivation, making it a valuable tool for enhancing exercise performance or lifting spirits during challenging times.

Music's impact on cognitive processes is also a key area of study. The "Mozart effect" is a well-known phenomenon suggesting that listening to classical music, particularly compositions by Mozart, can temporarily enhance spatial-temporal reasoning skills. While the extent and underlying mechanisms of this effect are still debated, it highlights the potential of music to influence cognitive functions such as memory, attention, and problem-solving.

The social and communicative aspects of music are equally important in the psychology of music. Music serves as a powerful means of social connection, facilitating bonding and cooperation among individuals. Group singing, for example, has been shown to enhance feelings of social cohesion and empathy. Music can also serve as a form of non-verbal communication, conveying emotions and intentions that words alone may struggle to express.

Understanding the psychology of music provides valuable insights into the ways music enriches our lives, enhances our well-being, and fosters connections with others. It highlights the profound and multifaceted nature of our relationship with music, affirming its place as an essential and cherished part of the human experience.

11

Chapter 11: The Globalization of Music

The globalization of music has led to an unprecedented exchange of musical styles, traditions, and influences across the world. Advances in communication technology, travel, and media have facilitated the blending of musical cultures, creating a rich and diverse global musical landscape.

One of the most significant drivers of musical globalization is the internet. Online platforms, such as YouTube, SoundCloud, and social media, have made it possible for artists from different corners of the world to share their music with a global audience. This accessibility has allowed for the discovery and appreciation of diverse musical genres, from K-pop and Afrobeat to reggae and flamenco. The internet has also enabled collaborations between artists from different cultural backgrounds, resulting in innovative and hybrid musical forms.

The impact of globalization on music is evident in the rise of world music festivals and events that celebrate cultural diversity. Festivals like WOMAD (World of Music, Arts and Dance) bring together musicians and audiences from around the globe, providing a platform for cross-cultural exchange and appreciation. These events highlight the universal language of music and its ability to bridge cultural divides.

Globalization has also led to the fusion of musical styles, creating new and exciting genres. For instance, Latin pop has gained immense popularity worldwide, blending traditional Latin rhythms with contemporary pop and electronic elements. Similarly, the genre of world fusion combines elements of traditional music from various cultures with modern genres like jazz, rock, and electronic music. These hybrid genres reflect the dynamic and interconnected nature of the global musical landscape.

However, the globalization of music also raises important questions about cultural appropriation and the preservation of musical heritage. While cross-cultural exchange can lead to creative innovation, it is essential to respect and honor the cultural contexts from which musical traditions originate. Efforts to preserve and promote indigenous and traditional music are crucial in ensuring that these rich and diverse cultural expressions are not lost in the process of globalization.

By exploring the globalization of music, we gain a deeper understanding of how music serves as a conduit for cultural exchange, innovation, and connection in an increasingly interconnected world.

12

Chapter 12: The Future of Music

As we look to the future, the world of music is poised for continued transformation and innovation. Technological advancements, changing cultural dynamics, and new modes of artistic expression will shape the musical landscape in ways we can only begin to imagine.

Artificial intelligence (AI) is set to play a significant role in the future of music creation and production. AI algorithms are already being used to compose music, generate unique soundscapes, and assist artists in the creative process. These technologies have the potential to push the boundaries of musical creativity, offering new possibilities for experimentation and collaboration. However, the role of AI in music also raises important ethical questions about authorship, originality, and the value of human creativity.

Virtual and augmented reality (VR/AR) are likely to redefine the way we experience music. Immersive VR concerts and interactive AR performances will offer audiences new and engaging ways to connect with music and artists. These technologies can create multisensory experiences that go beyond traditional live performances, providing a sense of presence and immersion that transcends physical boundaries.

The future of music distribution and consumption will continue to evolve with advancements in streaming technology and data analytics. Personalized music recommendations, based on sophisticated algorithms and user preferences, will become even more accurate and tailored. Blockchain technology may also play a role in transforming the music industry, offering new ways to manage copyright, royalties, and artist compensation.

Cultural and social trends will influence the themes and messages of future music. As global awareness of social and environmental issues grows, artists are likely to address these topics in their work, using music as a platform for advocacy and change. The diversity of voices and perspectives in the music industry will continue to expand, reflecting the evolving cultural landscape and promoting inclusivity and representation.

Ultimately, the future of music will be shaped by the ever-evolving relationship between artists, audiences, and technology. While the specific directions and innovations are unpredictable, one thing is certain: music will remain a vital and cherished part of the human experience, continuing to inspire, connect, and transform lives for generations to come.

13

Chapter 13: Music and Identity

Music plays a profound role in shaping and expressing individual and collective identities. It serves as a powerful medium through which people can explore, define, and communicate who they are. From personal playlists to cultural anthems, music reflects and influences the way we perceive ourselves and relate to the world around us.

At the individual level, music preferences often serve as a form of self-expression. The songs we choose to listen to can convey our moods, beliefs, and experiences. Music can provide a sense of comfort and validation, helping us navigate our emotions and identity. For instance, an adolescent may find solace in the lyrics of a song that resonates with their personal struggles, or an adult may use music to connect with their cultural heritage.

Collectively, music can foster a sense of belonging and unity. National anthems, protest songs, and genre-specific communities exemplify how music can unite people with shared values, experiences, and goals. For example, the punk rock movement of the 1970s and 1980s provided a voice for youth disillusioned with mainstream culture, creating a vibrant subculture centered around the music's rebellious spirit. Similarly, the rise of hip-hop in the Bronx during the 1970s brought together marginalized communities, giving them a platform to express their realities and aspirations.

Music also serves as a bridge between generations and cultures. Traditional music and folk songs often carry the stories and values of past generations, preserving cultural heritage and passing it down to future ones. Contemporary artists frequently draw on these traditions, blending them with modern influences to create new forms of musical expression that resonate with diverse audiences. This interplay between the old and the new enriches our understanding of identity and highlights the dynamic nature of culture.

By exploring the relationship between music and identity, we gain insight into the ways in which music shapes our sense of self and our connections with others. Music becomes a mirror that reflects our inner worlds and a conduit for expressing our place within the broader tapestry of human experience.

14

Chapter 14: Music and Healing

The healing power of music has been recognized for centuries, with ancient cultures using music as a therapeutic tool to promote physical, emotional, and spiritual well-being. Today, the field of music therapy continues to explore the ways in which music can support healing and enhance the quality of life for individuals across various contexts.

Music therapy involves the intentional use of music by trained professionals to achieve specific therapeutic goals. These goals may include reducing stress and anxiety, improving mood and emotional regulation, enhancing cognitive function, and fostering social connections. Music therapists work with diverse populations, including children with developmental disorders, individuals with mental health conditions, patients undergoing medical treatments, and elderly individuals with dementia.

One of the key mechanisms behind the therapeutic effects of music is its ability to regulate the autonomic nervous system. Listening to soothing music can activate the parasympathetic nervous system, promoting relaxation and reducing stress. Conversely, engaging in rhythmic activities, such as drumming or dancing, can stimulate the sympathetic nervous system, increasing alertness and energy levels. This dual capacity makes music a versatile tool for addressing a wide range of physiological and psychological needs.

In addition to its physiological effects, music has a profound impact on emotional well-being. It can evoke and process emotions that may be difficult to express verbally. For individuals experiencing trauma or grief, music therapy provides a safe and supportive environment for exploring and expressing their feelings. Familiar songs and melodies can also trigger positive memories and associations, offering comfort and a sense of continuity.

The use of music in healthcare settings has shown promising results in improving patient outcomes. For example, studies have found that music therapy can reduce pain perception and the need for analgesics in surgical patients, enhance motor function in individuals with stroke or Parkinson's disease, and improve social interaction and communication in children with autism spectrum disorder.

By harnessing the healing power of music, therapists and healthcare professionals can support individuals in their journey toward well-being and recovery. Music becomes a source of solace, empowerment, and connection, enriching the therapeutic experience and enhancing the overall quality of life.

15

Chapter 15: The Philosophy of Music

The philosophy of music explores the fundamental questions and concepts that underpin our understanding of music as an art form. It delves into the nature of music, its aesthetic qualities, and its significance in human life. Philosophers have long been fascinated by music, seeking to unravel its mysteries and uncover its deeper meanings.

One of the central questions in the philosophy of music is the nature of musical beauty. What makes a piece of music beautiful or moving? Some philosophers argue that musical beauty lies in the structure and harmony of the composition, while others emphasize the emotional and experiential aspects of music. The debate over the objective versus subjective nature of musical beauty reflects broader philosophical discussions about the nature of art and aesthetics.

The concept of musical meaning is another key area of inquiry. Does music have inherent meaning, or is its meaning entirely dependent on the listener's interpretation? Some philosophers, like Leonard Meyer, argue that music has an intrinsic syntax and semantics, akin to language, which can convey specific emotions and ideas. Others, like Susanne Langer, propose that music is a form of symbolic expression that communicates emotions and experiences in ways that language cannot fully capture.

The philosophy of music also examines the role of music in society and culture. Music has been viewed as a powerful force for social cohesion, moral education, and personal development. Plato, for example, believed that music had the capacity to shape an individual's character and influence the moral fabric of society. In contrast, Friedrich Nietzsche celebrated music as a manifestation of the primal and creative impulses of life, capable of transcending conventional morality and societal norms.

The relationship between music and time is another intriguing philosophical topic. Music unfolds in time, with rhythms, melodies, and harmonies creating a temporal experience that can evoke a sense of motion, tension, and resolution. Philosophers like Henri Bergson and Paul Ricoeur have explored how music reflects and shapes our perception of time, emphasizing its role in creating a temporal narrative and a sense of continuity.

By engaging with the philosophy of music, we gain a deeper appreciation of its complexities and nuances. Music is not merely a form of entertainment but a profound and multifaceted phenomenon that touches the very essence of what it means to be human. It invites us to reflect on our experiences, question our assumptions, and seek meaning in the world around us.

Brainwaves and Beats: Exploring the Neuroscience and Anthropology of Music

Dive into a captivating journey that melds the intricate workings of the human brain with the rich tapestry of global musical traditions. In "Brainwaves and Beats," we explore the profound and multifaceted relationship between music and humanity, from its earliest origins to its cutting-edge advancements.

Through twelve enlightening chapters, this book delves into the origins of music, the neuroscience behind music perception, and the powerful emotional connections that music fosters. We uncover how music has evolved alongside human societies, shaping cultural identities and social bonds. The intricate dance between music and rhythm is examined, shedding light on the cognitive and neural processes that underpin our sense of timing and coordination.

The book also ventures into the therapeutic potential of music, showcasing its ability to heal and enhance well-being across various contexts. From the early bone flutes to the digital synthesizers of today, the evolution of musical

CHAPTER 15: THE PHILOSOPHY OF MUSIC

instruments is traced, highlighting human creativity and innovation. The interplay between music and dance is explored, revealing how these two art forms create immersive and emotional experiences.

As we journey through the psychology of music, the globalization of musical traditions, and the philosophical inquiries into musical beauty and meaning, we gain a deeper appreciation of music's role in shaping our identities and experiences. "Brainwaves and Beats" is not just a book about music; it's a celebration of the universal language that transcends cultural boundaries and connects us all.

Perfect for music lovers, neuroscientists, anthropologists, and anyone curious about the intersection of art and science, this book invites you to explore the transformative power of music and its enduring impact on the human experience.

www.ingramcontent.com/pod-product-compliance
Lightning Source LLC
LaVergne TN
LVHW010443070526
838199LV00066B/6162